DIPLOMA OF JOANNITES:
Letter to the Knights Hospitaller

Bela IV, King of Hungary

Translated by: D.P. Curtin

DIPLOMA OF JOANNITES

Copyright @ 2023 Dalcassian Press

All rights reserved. No part of this publication may be reproduced, distributed, or transmitted in any form or by any means, including photocopying, recording, or other electronic or mechanical methods, without the prior written permission of the publisher, except in the case of brief quotations embodied in critical reviews and certain other non-commercial uses permitted by copyright law. For permission request, write to Dalcassian Press at dalcassianpublishing at gmail.com

ISBN: 979-8-8693-7825-5 (Paperback)

Library of Congress Control Number:
Author: Curtin, D.P. (1985-)

Printed by Ingram Content Group, 1 Ingram Blvd, La Vergne, Tennessee

First printing edition 2023.

DIPLOMA OF JOANNITES

DIPLOMA OF JOANNITES

DIPLOMA OF THE JOANNITES

The same Bela gives to the Hospitallers the most extensive lands of Zeurinus.

In the name of the Holy Trinity, and of the individual Unity. Amen. Bela, by the grace of God, King forever of Hungary, Dalmatia, Croatia, Rama, Seruia, Galicia, Lodomeria, and Cumania. The highness of kings requires, and it is due to the dignity of the sublime, that among other things he should strive more diligently for the multiplication of his subjects, by which their glory is more especially exalted in the multitude of the subject people; especially since the power, peace, and security of all kings and kingdoms are acknowledged to consist in the strength of their subjects. It is added, nevertheless, not a small part of the king's concern, to regard them more kindly, and to pursue them with greater favors, in whose persons and temporal life is hoped to be found, and the King of all kings is more inclined to be honored.

These, therefore, brought into consideration, together with the venerable man Rembald, the great teacher of the hospital houses of Jerusalem in the parts of Cismontane (al. Cismarinis) our beloved friend, upon the devastation of our kingdom, which by the hostile incursion of a barbarous nation called the Tartars, as in the loss of property, so of the inhabitants In the meantime he has greatly borne the expense, after a long negotiation with the princes and barons of our kingdom, in this rests our common deliberation, viz., that the same teacher, under the name of the house of the hospital, to take arms in support of our kingdom with a view to the defense of the Christian faith, according to the form annotated below, and He voluntarily bound himself and the house of the hospital to spend counsel and aid in our desolate country, in good faith, and also to submit to other conditions, inserted a little after the present ones; we give and confer upon him, and through him the whole of the said house the land of Zeurinus, with the Alps belonging to it, and all the other appurtenances, together with the Kenazates of Ioannis and Farcasius up to the river Olta, except the land of Kenaratus Lyrtioy (Pr. Linioy) of Waiwoda, which we leave to the Olahis, as they have hitherto held them; so, however, that we reserve half of all the benefits and incomes and securities from the whole land of Zeurin mentioned, and those belonging to the above-mentioned Kenazates, to us and our successors, with the other half yielding to the owner of the above-mentioned houses, except for the churches built and under construction, in all the above-mentioned lands. of whose revenues we should reserve nothing for ourselves; yet with respect to the reverences and rights of archbishops and bishops, which they are recognized to have; with the exception also of all mills, which have been made, or are being made, in any place, within the limits of the pre-mentioned lands; except within Lytira (Pr. Lytua) and also with all the buildings and farms, made by the taking of the so-called house of the brothers; also for the pastures of their animals and cattle; of pools also, which are now or will be made by them; all of which we wish to be retained in an integral manner for the sake of their brothers; besides the fisheries of the Danube and the pool of Cheley (Pr. Cheleg) which we reserve for ourselves and for them.

We have also agreed that half of all the profits and benefits which are collected from the Olahis, the inhabitants of the land of Litira, except the land of Hotsat (Pr. Harsot) with its appurtenances, shall be collected by the king, the house of the aforesaid hospital. We also desire that the aforesaid Olahi should assist the aforesaid brothers with their warlike equipment for the defense of the land, and to repulse the injuries, or to avenge them, which may be inflicted by foreigners, not subject to our dominion, they are obliged to spend according to their means. For these things, concerning the salt, which we grant to be sufficiently brought to the surface of the said land, and of those parts towards Bulgaria,

Greece, and Cumania, from whatever salt mines of Vltrasiluan, taken by us and the common people, may be extracted more conveniently, I grant in all respects the episcopal law, and not only the money which, according to the royal will and the counsel of the tutor of that house, should run for the appointed time, let us reserve one-half for ourselves, as has been said before about the other revenues; the other half of the said house to be turned over, to save the rights of the churches. The regulations which he granted to the nobles and others, both over their liberties, and over the judgments to inhabit the land already mentioned, to those coming from elsewhere, save our part of the revenues and benefits of those coming from thence, the so-called house; nor shall we have the opinions which he took upon them approved and firm; with this added, that if any sentence concerning the shedding of blood has been brought forward against the elders of the land, in which they feel that they are aggrieved, they may appeal to our court; adding this further, that if the army should attempt to invade our kingdom, which is far away, the fifth part of the armed men of the land already mentioned for the defense of our land should be bound to proceed to war in our army; but if we move an army towards Bulgaria, Greece, and Cumania.

A third of all those capable of war will go forward, and the house already mentioned will receive a portion of the acquisitions, both movable and immovable, in proportion to the number of persons in the army of Zeurinus, as well as the weapons. To these things we contributed to the aforesaid Preceptor, and through him, to the house of the hospital, from the river Olta and the Alps of Vltrasiluan, the whole of Cumania under the same conditions as were expressed above of the land of Zeurinus, except the land of Szeneslai Woiavoda Olahor, which we left to them, as they had hitherto held it; under the same conditions also for all that is ordered above concerning the land of Lytira. Now we do not wish to pass over this, that from the first entry of the oft-mentioned brothers until twenty-five years ago, all the revenue of the land of Cumania, the house already aforesaid should receive integrally; with the exception of the aforesaid land of Szeneslai, of which he will obtain only half of the income and benefits. From that time, however, half of all the proceeds, benefits, and services were administered to the royal treasury by the brothers of the same house, approved and sworn by the royal majesty; so, however, that from five years to five years, through our special person, his own income, services, and benefits, proceeding from thence, must be calculated; but those who will be kept in the camps or fortifications are taken, as they should be common to us and to our brothers, with health and other conditions on our part, and exceptions on the part of the hospital house in the land of Cumania, for example, concerning the churches, the mills, and all other things which They are described above in detail about Zeurinus. In order also to build a camp in the said land of Cumania, and not only against any assailants of the land of Cumania, but we will also expend the counsel and strength of the brothers themselves, as far as was necessary, and we were required by the brothers themselves; even by stopping the interference of others, by approaching there personally.

We also grant them the land of five hundred (Pr. 400.) ploughs, in Feketig, or elsewhere beyond the woods we will complete this number, where we shall find it more convenient for the said brothers to enter the land of Cumana or Zeurin; on which donation we will give our special letters. Finally, in order that the oft-mentioned house of hospital might be more conveniently able to procure for itself the necessaries by sea, for the conveniences of our kingdom and its own, we assigned to it the city of Scardona, near the sea, with all its appurtenances and rights, adjoining it; nor did the estate of Peczath (Pr. Pegzath) with its boundaries and uses, as our dearest brother, King Colomanus of illustrious memory , held; and how they belong to the estate itself; for the protection of the rights of the churches in the same.

Moreover, he also held land called Woyla (Pr. Waila) near the Danube not far from Zemilen, freed from the castle of Crassou, with all its appurtenances, as Nicholas, the brother of Vgolinus, held in perpetuity. We have contributed to the aforementioned brothers. Moreover, the oft-mentioned Master, in consequence of our concessions, which we make, or have made, for the causes written below, bound himself in the name of the said house, to take up arms against all pagans, of whatever nation, and not even against the Bulgarians; and against other Schismatics, if they should attempt to encroach on the kingdom, or on the borders of the kingdom, by name and precisely to introduce into our kingdom at present, for our and our kingdom's servants, one hundred brothers, decently and well prepared with military weapons and horses; and against the Christian army, desiring to enter our kingdom, he bound himself in the name of the said house, to give fifty armed brothers for the guard and defense of the camps and fortifications existing on the frontiers; That is, Posonium, Musunium, Suprunium, the Iron Castle, the new castle, and even below, wherever the king chooses to place it, and sixty against the Tartars, if they happen to enter our kingdom; which is absent. To all these, as long as they are in the custody of the camp and the fortifications, the royal provision will cause the necessary services to be taken. It is also added to the name of the house, that the preceptor or master, who for the time being to govern the houses existing in our kingdoms, is sent from overseas or other parts, is bound to promise at his entrance, given a faith according to the custom of his Order, all fidelity to the king and the kingdom; and to observe and pay attention to himself and his own, without deception, in all the above-mentioned things; and that he will give care and attention to populate not only the said lands, but also other lands of our kingdom; and that they do not receive peasants from our kingdom of whatever condition and nationality, and Saxons or Teutons from our kingdom, to inhabit the aforesaid lands, except by special permission from the king. It was further added by us, and by the aforesaid Preceptor, received in the name of the aforesaid house, that if the premises or any, or anything of the premises, to which the said Preceptor had committed himself and the aforesaid house, through him or through another preceptor or teacher; for the time appointed, should happen to be omitted, and the third solemnly admonished not to take care to satisfy, and the great overseas Master having been sufficiently requisitioned above these in the manner due for the royal part, would not make amends within a year after the requisition had been made, which had been omitted or neglected by the said master or instructor, for the time being existing, compensation or change by subtraction of income; or in another way, according to the quantity and quality of the excess, the royal deliberation will receive it, according to the good pleasure of his will.

Therefore, may the above-mentioned verses and particulars, recited before us and our barons, obtain the strength of perpetual firmness, as far as it is from our person; which by the faith given by the extension of our royal right hand, we promised, by lasting obligations, made on the part of the house, to observe inviolably, and to do so, we have delivered the present page, with the seal of our golden community; and the oft-mentioned Preceptor, under the name of the aforesaid house of hospital, by our beloved and faithful master Achilles, the Provost of Albense, the Vice-Chancellor of our court, we caused to be introduced into the physical possession of the aforesaid by royal authority.

DIPLOMA OF JOANNITES

Given by the hands of the Reverend Father Benedict, Archbishop of Coloque, and the Chancellor of our court. Father Stephen, archbishop of Strigon. Bartholomaeus Quinque-Eccles. Stephen of Zagreb Basilio Cenadien Pouza Bosnen. Arnoldus Jaurien. Zalando Wesprimien Vincent Warad. Heymone Wacien Go to Gallo. Lampert to the bishops of Agrien, who are successfully governing the churches of God. Ratislaus, the illustrious leader of Gaul, and the ban of all Sclavonia; Stephen, Count Palatine; Lawrence Waywoda Transilu Dionysius the teacher of Tauernicus. and the Count of Posonii; Rolando, judge of our court; Maurice, master of the Dapifers, and Count of Nitra; Chak, the master of Agazon and the count of Supruni; Bagin (al. Bagono), master of the butlers, and count of Bana; Paul of Zounuk; Benedict Musun Nicholas Zaladien. to another Nicholas of the iron castle; Henry Simighiensi, Seueric (Pr. Seuerinus) Counts of Alben, and others holding more than several Counties and Magistrates of our kingdom.

Year from the Incarnation of the Lord 1247, the fourth (al. III.) on the ninth of June, and in the twelfth year of our reign.

LATIN TEXT

DIPLOMA OF JOANNITES

Idem Bela Hospitalariis terras amplissimas de Zeurino confert.

In nomine sanctae Trinitatis, et individuae Unitatis. Amen. Bela, Dei gratia, Ungariae, Dalmatiae, Croatiae, Ramae, Seruiae, Galiciae, Lodomeriae, Cumaniaeque Rex in perpetuum. Regum Celsitudo requirit, et sublimium dignitati debetur, ut inter cetera eo studiosius ad multiplicationem inuigilet subditorum, quo ipsorum gloria in subiectae plebis multitudine specialius exaltatur; praesertim cum regum omnium et regnorum potentia, pax, et securitas, in suorum robore consistere dignoscantur. Accedit nihilominus non ad modicam sollicitudinis regiae partem, eos benignioribus intueri, et amplioribus prosequi beneficiis, in quorum personis et vtilitas temporalis prouenire speratur, et Rex regum omnium propensius honoratur. Hae itaque consideratione inducti, cum venerabili viro Rembaldo, domorum hospitalis Ierosolymitani magno praeceptore in partibus cismontanis (al. cismarinis) dilecto Amico nostro, super populatione regni nostri, quod per hostilem barbarae nationis incursum, quae Tartari appellantur, sicut in bonorum amissione, sic incolarum interemtione graue sustinuit dispendium, longo praehabito tractatu cum Principibus et baronibus regni nostri, in hoc nostra resedit communiter deliberatio, vt, quia idem praeceptor, nomine domus hospitalis, in subsidium regni nostri intuitu defensionis fidei Christianae, arma assumere, secundum formam inferius annotatam, et in populanda terra nostra consilium et auxilium impendere, bona fide, nec non alias subire conditiones, paullo post praesentibus insertas, se ac domum hospitalis sponte obligauit; damus, et conferimus sibi, et per eum dictae domui *totam terram de Zeurino,* cum alpibus ad eam pertinentibus, et aliis attinentiis omnibus, pariter cum Kenazatibus Ioannis et Farcasii vsque ad fluuium *Oltae,* excepta terra Kenaratus Lyrtioy (Pr. Linioy) Waiwodae, quam Olahis relinquimus, prout iidem hactenus tenuerunt; ita tamen, quod medietatem omnium vtilitatum et redituum, ac seruitiorum de tota terra Zeurini memorata, et Kenazatibus supra nominatis prouenientium, nobis et successoribus nostris reseruamus, medietate alia ad vsum domus supra dictae cedente, exceptis ecclesiis constructis et construendis, in omnibus terris supradictis, de quarum reditibus nihil nobis reseruamus; saluis tamen reuerentiis et iuribus archiepiscoporum, et episcoporum, quae habere dignoscuntur; exceptis etiam molendinis omnibus, infra terminos praenotatarum terrarum vbicunque factis, vel faciendis; praeterquam intra Lytira (Pr. Lytua) nec non aedificiis et agriculturis omnibus, sumtibus fratrum dictae domus factis; foenetis quoque, seu animalium et pecorum suorum pascuis; piscinis etiam, quae nunc sunt vel fient per ipsos; quae omnia ad ipsorum fratrum vsum integraliter volumus retineri; praeter piscationes Danubii ac piscinae de Cheley (Pr. Cheleg) quas nobis et ipsis communes reseruamus. Contulimus etiam, quod medietatem omnium prouentuum et vtilitatum, quae ab Olahis, terram Lityra habitantibus, excepta terra Hotsat (Pr. Harsot) cum pertinentibus suis, regi colligentur, domus hospitalis percipiat antedicta. Volumus etiam, quod memorati Olahi ad defensionem terrae, et ad iniurias propulsandas, seu vlciscendas, quae ab extraneis, nostrae ditioni non subiectis, inferentur, iam dictis fratribus cum apparatu suo bellico assistere, et e conuerso ipsi fratres in casibus consimilibus eis subsidium et iuuamen iuxta posse impendere teneantur. Ad haec de salibus, quos ad vsum dictae terrae, et illarum partium versus Bulgariam, Graeciam, et Cumaniam sufficienter deferri concedimus, de quacunque salis fodina Vltrasiluana commodius, sumtibus nobis et ipsis communibus, extrahi potuerint, saluo in omnibus iure episcopali, nec non de moneta, quae illic de voluntate regia et consilio praeceptoris domus illius, pro tempore constituti, curret, medietatem nobis reseruamus, sicuti de ceteris reditibus est praetactum; medietate alia ad vsum dictae domus conuertenda, saluis iuribus ecclesiarum. Ordinationes, quas nobilibus ac aliis tam super libertatibus ipsorum, quam super iudiciis ad inhabitandam terram iam dictam, aliunde venientibus concesserit, salua parte nostra redituum et vtilitatum inde prouenientium, dicta domus; nec non sententias, quas tulerit in eosdem, ratas habebimus atque firmas; hoc addito, quod si contra maiores terrae aliqua sententia de sanguinis effusione prolata fuerit, in qua senserint se grauari, ad nostram curiam valeant appellare; hoc insuper adiecto, quod si exercitus regnum nostrum, quod absit, inuadere attemptaret, quinta pars armatorum terrae iam dictae pro defensione terrae nostrae in exercitu nostro ad bella procedere teneatur; si autem versus Bulgariam, Graeciam et Cumaniam exercitum mouerimus; tertia pars omnium ad bella habilium praecedet, et de aquisitionibus tam mobilium, quam immobilium portionem recipiet domus iam dicta, pro numero personarum exercitus de Zeurino pariter et armorum. Ad haec contulimus Praeceptori antedicto et per ipsum domui hospitalis a fluuio Oltae et alpibus vltrasiluanis totam Cumaniam sub eisdem conditionibus, quae de terra de Zeurino superius sunt expressae, excepta terra Szeneslai Woiavodae Olahorum, quam eisdem reliquimus, prout iidem hactenus tenuerunt; sub eisdem etiam conditionibus per omnia, quae de terra Lytira sunt superius ordinatae. Hoc autem nolumus praeterire, quod a primo introitu saepe dictorum fratrum vsque ad viginti quinque annos omnes reditus Cumaniae terrae, integraliter domus percipiat iam praefata; praeterquam de terra Szeneslai antedicta, de qua tantum medietatem redituum et vtilitatum obtinebit. Ex tunc vero medietas omnium prouentuum, vtilitatum et seruitiorum per fratres eiusdem domus, a celsitudine regia approbatos et iuratos, fisco regio ministratur; ita tamen, quod de quinquennio in quinquennium per nostrum hominem specialem proprii reditus, seruitia et vtilitates, exinde prouenientes, debeant computari; sumtus vero, qui in castrorum, seu munitionum custodiis fient, sicut nobis et ipsis fratribus debent esse communes, saluis aliis conditionibus pro parte nostra, et exceptionibus pro parte domus hospitalis in terra Cumaniae, vt puta de Ecclesiis, de molendiuis et aliis omnibus, quae singillatim superius de Zeurino sunt expressa. Ad castra etiam aedificanda in dicta terra Cumaniae, nec non contra quoslibet impugnatores terrae Cumanae consilium et vires ipsis fratribus impendemus, quum necesse fuerit, et ab ipsis fratribus fuerimus requisiti; etiam cessantibus impedimentis aliis, illuc personaliter accedendo. Concedimus etiam eisdem terram quingentorum (Pr. 400.) aratrorum in Feketig, vel alibi vltra siluas complebimus hunc numerum, vbi magis ad introitum terrae Cumanae vel Zeurini dictis fratribus videbimus expedire; super qua donatione litteras nostras dabimus speciales. Denique, vt saepe dicta domus hospitalis commodius sibi necessaria per mare valeat procurare, pro vtilitatibus regni nostri et suis, contulimus sibi iuxta maritima ciuitatem Scardonam, cum omnibus suis pertinentiis et iuribus, ipsam contingentibus; nec non praedium Peczath (Pr. Pegzath) cum suis terminis et vtilitatibus, prout charissimus frater noster, inclytae memoriae *Colomanus* rex tenuit; et quemadmodum ad ipsum praedium pertinere digoscuntur; saluis ecclesiarum iuribus in eisdem. Insuper etiam terram nomine Woyla (Pr. Waila) iuxta Danubium non longe a Zemilen existentem, a castro de Crassou exemtam, cum omnibus pertinentiis et vtilitatibus suis, sicut Nicolaus, frater Vgolini, in perpetuitatibus tenuerat; fratribus contulimus praedictis. Porro saepedictus Praeceptor ob concessiones nostras, quas propter caussas infra scriptas facimus, seu fecimus, obligauit se nomine dictae domus, arma assumere contra omnes paganos, cuiuscunque nationis, nec non contra Bulgaros; contra alios autem Schismaticos, si regnum, aut regni confinia inuadere attemptarent, nominatim ac praecise introducere in regnum nostrum in praesente, ad nostrum et regni nostri seruitium centum fratres, militaribus armis et equis decenter, et bene praeparatos; contra exercitum autem Christianorum, regnum nostrum intrare volentem, obligauit se nomine dictae domus, dare quinquaginta fratres armatos ad custodiam et defensionem castrorum et munitionum in confiniis existentium; Vt est Posonium, Musunium, Suprunium, Castrum ferreum, castrum nouum et etiam infra, vbicunque rex voluerit collocare, et sexaginta contra Tartaros, si regnum nostrum ipsos intrare contingat; quod absit. Quibus omnibus, quamdiu sunt in custodiis castrorum et munitionum, regia prouisio faciet sumtus necessarios ministrare. Adiunctum est etiam nomine domus, quod praeceptor seu magister, qui pro tempore ad gubernationem domorum in regnis nostris existentium, mittetur de partibus transmarinis vel aliis, in introitu suo promittere teneatur, data fide iuxta consuetudinem sui Ordinis, omnem fidelitatem regi et regno; et obseruare facere atque attendere in se et suis, sine fraude, vniuersa et singula supra dicta; et quod curam et operam dabit, ad populandum non solum dictas terras, sed etiam alias terras regni nostri; et quod rusticos de regno nostro cuiuscunque conditionis et nationis, ac Saxones vel Teutonicos de nostro regno non recipiant ad habitandum terras supradictas, nisi de licentia regit speciali. Adiunctum insuper fuit a nobis, et a Praeceptore iam dicto, nomine praefatae domus receptum, quod si praemissa vel aliqua, seu aliquid de praemissis, ad quae dictus Praeceptor se et praedictam domum superius obligauerat, per ipsum vel per alium praeceptorem seu magistrum; pro tempore constitutum, omitti contingeret, et tertio sollempniter admonitus satisfacere non curaret, magnusque Magister transmarinus super haec modo debito pro parte regia sufficienter requisitus, non emendaret infra annum post factam requisitionem, quod omissum est seu neglectum per dictum magistrum, seu praeceptorem, pro tempore existentem, emendam seu vltionem per subtractionem redituum; vel alio modo, iuxta quantitatem et qualitatem excessus, regia deliberatio recipiet, iuxta suae beneplacitum voluntatis. Vt igitur vniuersa et singula supradicta, coram nobis et baronibus nostris recitata, perpetuae firmitatis, quantum est ex persona nostra, robur obtineant; quae fide data porrectione dexterae regalis nostrae promisimus, durantibus obligationibus, ex parte domus factis, inuiolabiliter obseruare, et facere obseruari, praesentem tradidimus paginam, charactere bullae nostrae aureae communitam; et saepe dictum Praeceptorem, nomine domus hospitalis praefatae, per dilectum, fidelem nostrum, magistrum Achillem, Albensem Praepositum, aulae nostrae vice-Cancellarium, in possessionem praedictorum corporalem auctoritate regia fecimus introduci. Datum per manus reuerendi Patris Benedicti Archiepiscopi Colocensis et aulae nostrae Cancellarii. Ven. Patre Stephano archiepiscopo Strigon. Bartholomaeo Quinque-Eccles.

Stephano Zagrab. Basilio Cenadien. Pouza Bosnen. Arnolpho Iaurien. Zalando Wesprimien. Wicentio Warad. Heymone Wacien. Gallo Transilu. Lamperto Agriensi Episcopis, ecclesias Dei feliciter gubernantibus. Ratislao illustri Duce Galliciae et bano totius Sclauoniae; Stephano Comite Palatino; Laurentio Waywoda Transilu. Dionysio magistro Tauernic. et Comite Posoniensi; Rolando iudice aulae nostrae; Mauritio magistro Dapiferorum, et Comite Nitriensi; Chak magistro Agazonum et comite Supruniensi; Bagin (al. Bagono) magistro pincernarum, et *comite de Bana;* Paulo de Zounuk; Benedicto Musun. Nicolao Zaladien. alio Nicolao de ferreo castro; Henrico Simighiensi, Seuerico (Pr. Seuerino) Albensi comitibus, et aliis quam pluribus Comitatus et Magistratus regni nostri tenentibus; anno ab Incarnatione Domini MCCXLVII. quarto (al. III.) nonas Iunii, regni autem nostri anno duodecimo."

The Scriptorium Project is the work of a small group of lay people of various apostolic churches who are interested in the preservation, transmission, and translation of the works of the early and medieval church. Our efforts are to make the works of the church fathers accessible to anyone who might have an interest in Christian antiquities and the theological, philosophical, and moral writings that have become the bedrock of Western Civilization.

To-date, our releases have pulled from the Greek, Syriac, Georgian, Latin, Celtic, Ethiopian, and Coptic traditions of Christianity, and have been pulled from sundry local traditions and languages.

DIPLOMA OF JOANNITES

DIPLOMA OF JOANNITES

ROMANO-HUNGARIAN CHURCH COLLECTION:

Diploma of the Joannites: Letter to the Knights Hospitaller
    Bela IV, King of Hungary- June 15, 2023
Charter of the Order of the Dragon
    Sigismund, King of Hungary- Jan. 1, 2024
The Golden Bull of 1224: Chart to the Transylvanian Saxons
    Andrew II, King of Hungary- Feb. 15, 2024
Charter of the Abbey of Tihany
    Andrew I, King of Hungary- May 15, 2024

www.ingramcontent.com/pod-product-compliance
Lightning Source LLC
LaVergne TN
LVHW052049070526
838201LV00086B/5177